AF597359

Willy,

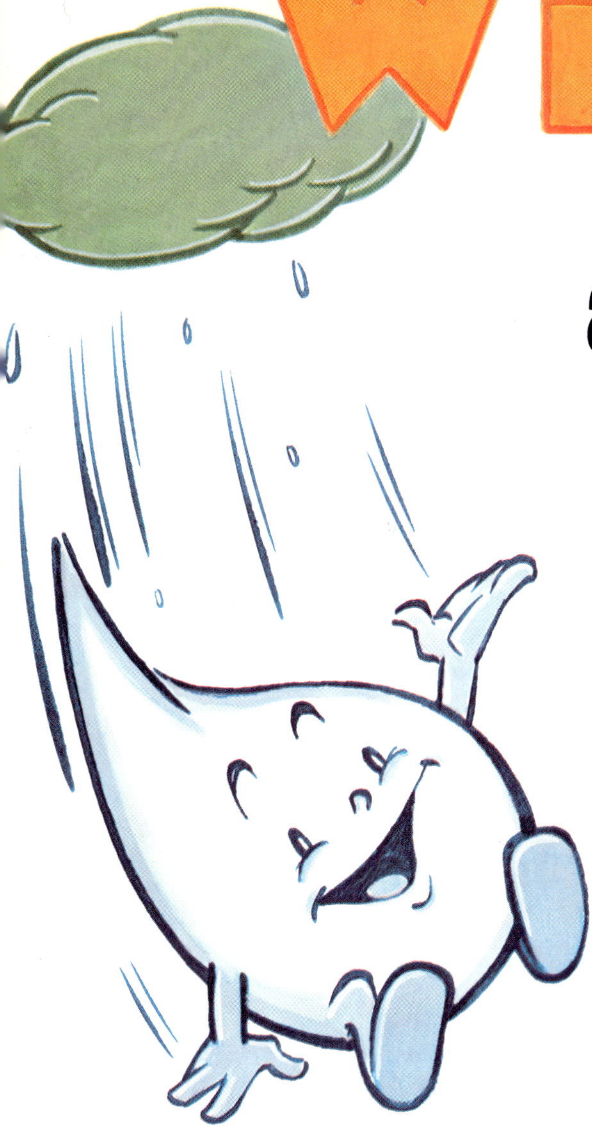

a story of water

Written by JEROME SPAR

Illustrated by BIL CONNOR

published by

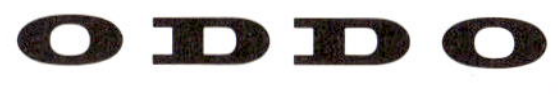

ODDO PUBLISHING

Fayetteville, Georgia

Symbol for exciting book ideas

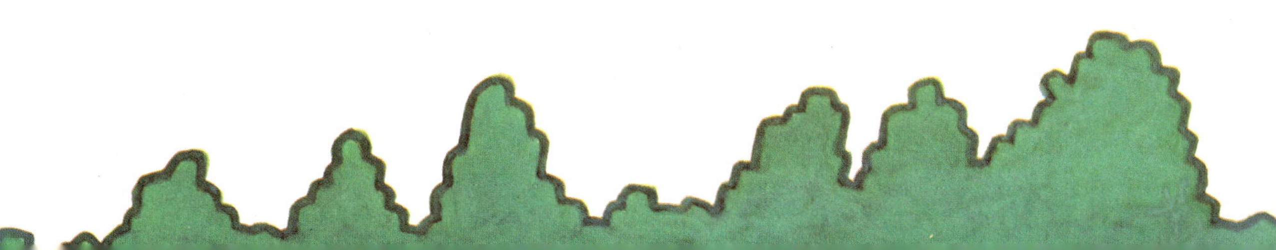

Dedicated to RICHARD, SUSAN and FRAN

managing editor

Genevieve Oddo

Advisers

Anita Bullard
Assistant Professor of English
Oswego State University College, New York

Ruth Foy
Library Coordinator
Baldwin-Whitehall Public Schools
Pittsburgh, Pennsylvania

Jean Henschel
President
Educational Research and Consultation Services
Tucson, Arizona

Norbert C. Lopez
Superintendent of Schools
Espanola, New Mexico

Nina Martin
Coordinator, ESEA Title II
Montgomery, Alabama

Rae Oetting
Member, Outdoor Writers of America

Mel Schumacher
Coordinator, General Curriculum
Monterey County Office of Education, California

Alvin M. Westcott
Associate Professor of Elementary Education
Oswego State University College, New York

Reading Consultant
William E. Jones
Director of Education
D'Youville College
Buffalo, New York

Library of Congress Catalog Card Number 68-56819.
Printed in the United States of America. Library Binding

I wrote this book for my daughter, Susan, when she was about eight years old. In it I tried to tell her about the many forms of water, and how water changes from one form to another as it moves around the world. These changes of water — from liquid to ice to unseen water vapor — are taking place around us all the time. They happen in the air, in the sea, in lakes and rivers, and in the earth itself. We call this cycle of changes the *water cycle,* and that is what the book is about. In this book we will follow some water through all its changing forms as it moves from place to place. To help you remember that it is always the same water, we have given it a name — WILLY.

Jerome Spar

This is the story of a drop of water which we have affectionately named Willy.

Willy's story has no beginning and no end. We may start the story anywhere.

But let's begin on a sunny, summer day when Willy is floating in the ocean, together with millions of other drops.

Willy has been floating in the ocean for a long time. He is quite salty.

For a while Willy was in the deep water where it is dark and cool.

Now he is on top of the water and he is being warmed by the heat from the sun.

Willy is beginning to feel very warm. He tingles.

Willy is made up of tiny pieces of water, called *molecules*.

When Willy tingles, his molecules begin to move around faster and faster.

What is happening to Willy?

Some of his molecules are beginning to fly away into the air. Now more molecules fly away. Willy, the water drop, is *evaporating*.

We cannot see him anymore.

His molecules are floating around in the air, but they are invisible.

Willy is no longer a drop of water.

He has turned into *water vapor*.

And he has left the salt behind him in the ocean.

We cannot see Willy now, but he is there, floating in the air.

The wind pushes him along.

Willy is traveling faster now.

He is flying over the ocean.

Willy, the vapor, is leaving the warm water.

Pushed by the wind, he is skimming to the north where the water and air are colder.

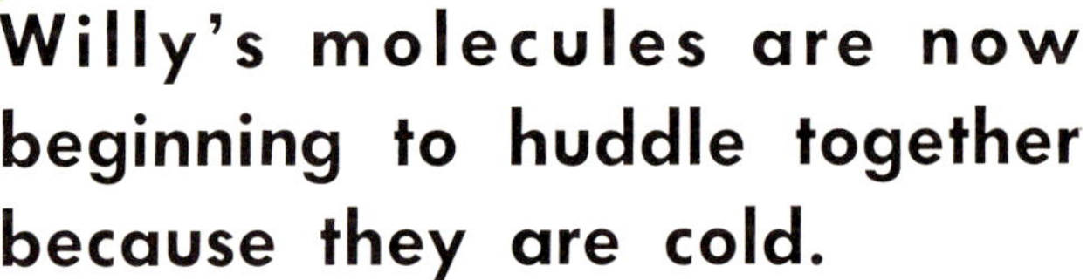

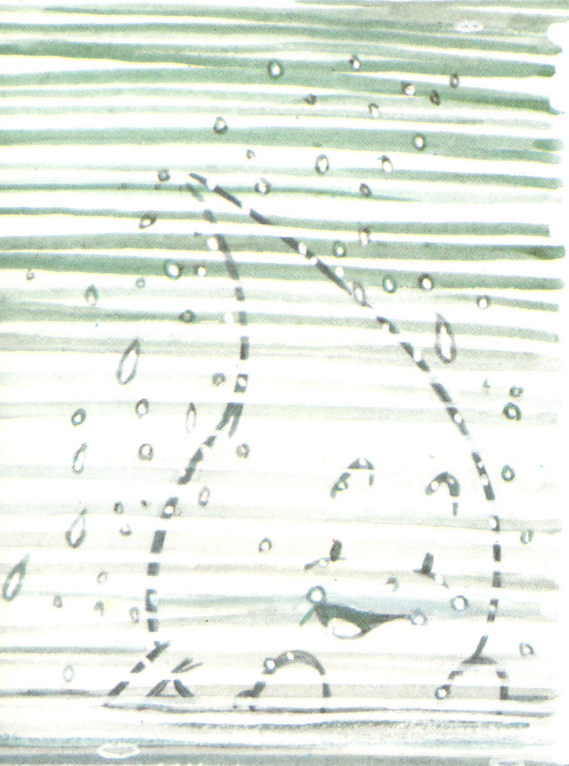

Willy's molecules are now beginning to huddle together because they are cold.

The colder he gets, the closer do Willy's molecules come together.

They are very close to each other now.

When water molecules come very close together, they form drops again. This is called *condensation*.

Look! You can see Willy now; but he is very wispy.

He is not one big drop.

He is a lot of tiny drops.

Willy is water again; but he looks like smoke.

Willy has become *fog*.

Boo-wum! Boo-wum!

That is a fog horn blowing.

A great ship is moving carefully through Willy's fog.

The captain cannot see through the fog.

He moves his ship slowly. He does not want to hit another ship.

Willy, the fog, is causing the captain a lot of trouble.

"Say! Stop that! Stop pushing!"

A strong wind is pushing Willy again.

The captain laughs. He is happy.

"The fog is lifting," says the captain, as Willy drifts away.

Willy is becoming warmer again.

The wind has pushed him over warmer water.

A narrow river of warm water flows through the Atlantic Ocean. It is called the *Gulf Stream*.

As Willy passes over the Gulf Stream he begins to tingle again.

His molecules are flying apart again.

Where is he? Can you see him?

He is disappearing. He is gone.

Willy has turned into water vapor once more.

The wind carries Willy over the land.

He swirls around the people, but they do not see him.

"Good morning, Mrs. Smith," says the man in the grocery store. "It's rather warm today."

"I don't mind the heat," says Mrs. Smith, "but I do not like this *humidity*. It is so damp."

Mrs. Smith is talking about Willy.

Humidity is the name people give to water vapor.

When there is a lot of water vapor in the air, no more water can evaporate. If you hang your clothes out to dry, they do not dry. The water on your skin does not evaporate either.

That is why you feel warm and uncomfortable. When the water on your skin evaporates, it draws heat from your skin. But if the air is full of water vapor, the water on your skin stays there and you feel warm. That is why people sometimes do not like Willy.

Now the wind is pushing Willy up the side of a mountain.

Higher and higher he climbs. Willy is very high now. As he climbs, Willy gets colder. His molecules are shivering. They are beginning to huddle together again.

Look there! Do you see a wisp of something? It is Willy. We can see him now.

Willy is no longer vapor. He is a lot of small drops of water, just as he was when he was fog.

Willy has become part of a cloud.

The wind is still pushing Willy higher and higher. Some of Willy's little drops start to fall. The wind catches them and pushes them up again. It is very cold now.

The molecules in the drops cannot keep warm. They huddle closer and closer.

What sparkles so brightly?

It looks like a piece of glass.

It is not glass; it is ice.

One of Willy's drops has turned into an *ice crystal.*

Now more and more of the drops are turning into ice.

The ice crystals sparkle in the sunlight.

They dance around gaily.

As they dance, Willy's ice crystals bump into each other. They cling together. Some of the crystals are getting quite large.

The ice crystals bump into the water drops and the drops freeze. This makes the ice crystals bigger.

See there! How beautifully that ice crystal has grown! It looks like a lacy star with six points. Willy has become a snowflake.

The air cannot hold Willy, the snowflake, up any longer. Willy is falling.

Turning and glistening, he tumbles down; he falls into a cloud. As he sinks through the cloud, Willy waves to all his friends, to all the drops and crystals.

He bumps into some of the cloud drops as he falls, and they cling to him. Willy grows as he falls.

Bigger, bigger, BIGGER. Willy is a giant snowflake now, and he falls fast.

Something strange is happening to Willy as he falls.

He is getting warmer. He is tingling again. His molecules are moving faster.

The pretty snowflake is changing. It is turning gray and wet.

The snowflake is gone. Willy has melted.

He is still falling through the cloud. But Willy is too warm to be a snowflake. He is a raindrop again.

Willy, the raindrop, bumps against other smaller drops in the cloud. Some of the drops cling to Willy as he falls, making Willy grow. He is a large drop now.

Splash! Willy has fallen into a puddle on the ground. He is high up on the mountainside.

More raindrops join Willy in the puddle. The drops bounce and splash.

Some of the water seeps into the ground. But Willy and most of his friends in the puddle slide into a small stream.

The stream carries Willy along. Down the mountainside trickles the stream, faster and faster. The stream tumbles along over rocks and branches.

It is cold in the stream, but not as cold as when Willy was a snowflake.

The stream is getting wider now. More streams flow into Willy's stream. The water rushes down the mountainside. The stream is moving very fast. There is a roaring noise.

The sky seems to be right in front of Willy. He is falling through space. Crash!

At the bottom of the waterfall Willy lands in a churning river. The river runs swiftly.

Pieces of mud from the river bank fall into the water. Willy is no longer clear and blue. He is yellow and brown with mud.

What is that big wall ahead? It is a dam. In the dam there is a huge wheel.

Willy and some other water drops are going to pass through the wheel.

They push the wheel as they force their way through. The wheel turns. The great wheel turns a dynamo which makes electricity. The electricity goes out in wires to the people who use it for light and power, to make toast, and for many other purposes.

Willy is tired. He worked hard to push through the wheel.

He floats lazily in the river below the dam. But once more he must be on his way, gliding down the river.

The lapping water splashes Willy onto the bank of the river. He sinks into the ground. For a long time Willy sinks deeper and deeper.

It is dark and cool under the ground. In the darkness Willy feels other drops pressing against him. They all move very slowly.

But now something is pulling the drops.

Willy and his friends are being pulled into a round pipe which sticks down into the earth.

Whoosh! Willy flies up the pipe, and out he comes.

A pump has pulled Willy out of the ground.

A little boy standing near the pump catches Willy in a pail.

He carries water to a garden where he spills it on the flowers. The water sinks into the soil again.

The thirsty roots of the flower plants suck in the water drops from the soil. The water is carried up the stem of the plant to the leaves. The water carries food to the hungry plant.

Now the plant has finished with Willy. Willy slips softly out of the plant through the leaves. Tiny droplets of water glisten on the leaves.

But soon they are gone and Willy is invisible again. Once more he is a vapor.

The wind picks Willy up and carries him far out to sea again. Willy passes over the warm Gulf Stream. The air is heated by the warm water.

The air feels light. It rises like a balloon. Willy is carried up with the air.

Once more the molecules huddle together as Willy gets colder and colder.

Do you see that wisp of cloud forming there?

That is Willy.

He has condensed again into small water drops.

The air rises swiftly. More and more drops form. The cloud looks like a cotton ball now. We call this kind of cloud a *cumulus* cloud.

The cumulus cloud continues to grow. Willy is carried up into the top of the cloud. He collects more drops around him and grows.

Willy is big now – too big for the air to hold him up any longer. He starts to fall. Willy is part of a rain shower.

The rain falls into the ocean.

Willy is back where he started.

He is becoming salty again.

How long do you think Willy will stay in the ocean this time?

DEFINITIONS

CLOUD: A lot of tiny water drops or ice crystals floating in the air close together.

CONDENSE: To change from a vapor to a liquid, as when dew forms on the grass at night.

CUMULUS CLOUD: A lumpy white cloud that looks like a ball of cotton or a head of cauliflower.

DAM: A big wall built to hold back a river.

DYNAMO: A machine that makes electricity. Some dynamos are driven by the water that passes through a dam.

EVAPORATE: To change from liquid into a vapor, as when dew vanishes from the grass after sunrise.

FOG: A cloud that is lying on the ground. You cannot see very far through a fog.

FREEZE: To change from liquid to solid, as when ice forms on a lake.

GAS: Matter that is neither solid nor liquid. Gases are lighter than solids and liquids. If you put a gas in a bottle, it will fill the whole bottle no matter how much you put in. Most gases, like air and water vapor, are invisible.

GULF STREAM: A vast warm ocean current flowing from the Gulf of Mexico northward through the Atlantic.

HUMIDITY: The amount of water vapor in the air.

ICE CRYSTAL: A small piece of solid water with many sides – usually six – that sparkles as it turns and twists because of the way light is reflected from its sides.

LIQUID: The wet form of water that we see all the time, as in a bathtub.

MELT: To change from solid to liquid, as when ice changes to running streams of water in the springtime.

MOLECULES: The invisible bits of matter of which all things are made. Each kind of matter, such as water, has its own special kind of molecules.

PUMP: A machine that sucks water up out of the ground or out of a well.

RAIN: Many large drops of liquid water falling to the earth from clouds.

ROOT: The part of a plant that is underground which absorbs water and food for the plant to live on.

SNOWFLAKE: A large ice crystal in the form of a star with six points that is made up of many small crystals, and which falls to the earth from clouds.

SOLID: Something hard that does not flow like a liquid or move around like a gas. Ice is a solid.

VAPOR: The invisible gas form of water that is always in the air although we cannot see it. (See Humidity)

about the author

JEROME SPAR has been Professor of Meteorology at New York University for more than fifteen years, interrupting his University teaching for one year, 1964-1965, to serve as Research Director of the United States Weather Bureau.

He received his Ph.D. in 1950 from New York University.

In World War II he served as Weather Officer, U.S.A.F., from 1942-1946.

Since 1943 Jerome Spar has been engaged in meteorological research and has authored many papers in scientific journals. He is the author of *The Way of the Weather*, and *Earth, Sea, and Air*.

He and his wife, Frances, have two children, Susan and Richard.

about the illustrator

Bill Connor was born in Elgin, Illinois and after his formal schooling, attended the Chicago Academy of Fine Arts.

His art background has taken him into all forms of illustration, working in Chicago Commercial Art Studios; Omaha Bee-News Art Department; in the Animation Department of Walt Disney Studios in California; for more than twenty years in the Art Department of Des Moines Register and Tribune, and for the same paper on several comic strips in their Syndicate Department, (a separate organization within the Cowles enterprises).

He is married and father of three sons.

In World War II he served in the Army for two years.

His hobbies consist of baseball, basketball, swimming, and bowling.